ELIZABETH
BARRETT BROWNING

Se l e c t e d
P o e m s

BLOOMSBURY
* POETRY *
CLASSICS

This selection by Ian Hamilton first published 1993
Copyright © 1993 by Bloomsbury Publishing Ltd

Bloomsbury Publishing Ltd, 2 Soho Square,
London WIV 5DE

A CIP catalogue record for this book is available from the
British Library

ISBN 0 7475 14933

10 9 8 7 6 5 4 3 2 1

Typeset by Hewer Text Composition Services Limited,
Edinburgh
Printed in Great Britain by St Edmundsbury Press, Suffolk
Bound in Great Britain by Hunter and Foulis Limited,
Edinburgh

CONTENTS

From LADY GERALDINE'S COURTSHIP
A Romance of the Age

*A poet writes to his friend. Place – A room in Wycombe
Hall. Time – Late in the evening.*

Dear my friend and fellow student,
   I would lean my spirit o'er you!
Down the purple of this chamber, tears should scarcely
   run at will.
I am humbled who was humble. Friend, – I bow my
   head before you.
You should lead me to my peasants, – but their faces
   are too still.

There's a lady – an earl's daughter, – she is proud and
   she is noble,
And she treads the crimson carpet, and she breathes
   the perfumed air,
And a kingly blood sends glances up her princely eye
   to trouble,
And the shadow of a monarch's crown is softened in
   her hair.

She has halls among the woodlands, she has castles by
  the breakers,
She has farms and she has manors, she can threaten
  and command,
And the palpitating engines snort in steam across her
  acres,
As they mark upon the blasted heaven the measure of
  the land.

There are none of England's daughters who can show
  a prouder presence;
Upon princely suitors praying, she has looked in her
  disdain.
She was sprung of English nobles, I was born of
  English peasants;
What was I that I should love her – save for
  competence to pain?

I was only a poor poet, made for singing at her
   casement,
As the finches or the thrushes, while she thought of
   other things.
Oh, she walked so high above me, she appeared to my
   abasement,
In her lovely silken murmur, like an angel clad in wings!

Many vassals bow before her as her carriage sweeps
   their doorways;
She has blest their little children, – as a priest or
   queen were she.
Far too tender, or too cruel far, her smile upon the
   poor was,
For I thought it was the same smile which she used to
   smile on *me*.

She has voters in the Commons, she has lovers in the
    palace;
And of all the fair court-ladies, few have jewels half as
    fine;
Oft the prince has named her beauty 'twixt the red
    wine and the chalice.
Oh, and what was *I* to love her? my beloved, my
    Geraldine!

Yet I could not choose but love her. I was born to
    poet-uses,
To love all things set above me, all of good and all of
    fair:
Nymphs of mountain, not of valley, we are wont to
    call the Muses
And in nympholeptic climbing, poets pass from mount
    to star.

And because I was a poet, and because the public
    praised me,
With a critical deduction for the modern writer's fault,
I could sit at rich men's tables, – though the courtesies
    that raised me,
Still suggested clear between us the pale spectrum of
    the salt.

And they praised me in her presence; – 'Will your
    book appear this summer?'
Then returning to each other – 'Yes, our plans are for
    the moors.'
Then with whisper dropped behind me – 'There he is!
    the latest comer!
Oh, she only likes his verses! what is over, she
    endures.'

'Quite low-born! self-educated! somewhat gifted though
  by nature, –
And we make a point of asking him, – of being very
  kind.
You may speak, he does not hear you! and besides, he
  writes no satire, –
All these serpents kept by charmers leave the natural
  sting behind.'

I grew scornfuller, grew colder, as I stood up there
  among them,
Till as frost intense will burn you, the cold scorning
  scorched my brow;
When a sudden silver speaking, gravely cadenced,
  over-rung them,
And a sudden silken stirring touched my inner nature
  through.

I looked upward and beheld her. With a calm and
   regnant spirit,
Slowly round she swept her eyelids, and said clear
   before them all –
'Have you such superfluous honour, sir, that able to
   confer it
You will come down, Mister Bertram, as my guest to
   Wycombe Hall?'

Here she paused, – she had been paler at the first
   word of her speaking,
But because a silence followed it, blushed somewhat, as
   for shame,
Then, as scorning her own feeling, resumed calmly – 'I
   am seeking
More distinction than these gentlemen think worthy
   of my claim.

'Ne'ertheless, you see, I seek it – not because I am a
    woman'
(Here her smile sprang like a fountain, and, so,
    overflowed her mouth),
'But because my woods in Sussex have some purple
    shades at gloaming
Which are worthy of a king in state, or poet in his
    youth.

'I invite you, Mister Bertram, to no scene for worldly
    speeches –
Sir, I scarce should dare – but only where God asked
    the thrushes first –
And if *you* will sing beside them, in the covert of my
    beeches,
I will thank you for the woodlands, . . . for the human
    world, at worst.'

Then she smiled around right childly, then she gazed
   around right queenly,
And I bowed – I could not answer; alternated light
   and gloom –
While as one who quells the lions, with a steady eye
   serenely,
She, with level fronting eyelids, passed out stately from
   the room.

Oh, the blessèd woods of Sussex, I can hear them still
   around me,
With their leafy tide of greenery still rippling up the
   wind.
Oh, the cursèd woods of Sussex! where the hunter's
   arrow found me,
When a fair face and a tender voice had made me mad
   and blind!

. . .

THE ROMANCE OF THE SWAN'S NEST

So the dreams depart,
So the fading phantoms flee,
And the sharp reality
Now must act its part.
                        Westwood's *Beads from a Rosary.*

I

Little Ellie sits alone
'Mid the beeches of a meadow,
    By a stream-side on the grass,
    And the trees are showering down
Doubles of their leaves in shadow,
    On her shining hair and face.

II

She has thrown her bonnet by,
And her feet she has been dipping
    In the shallow water's flow;
    Now she holds them nakedly
In her hands, all sleek and dripping,
    While she rocketh to and fro.

III

Little Ellie sits alone,
And the smile she softly uses,
  Fills the silence like a speech,
  While she thinks what shall be done, –
And the sweetest pleasure chooses
  For her future within reach.

IV

Little Ellie in her smile
Chooses . . . 'I will have a lover,
  Riding on a steed of steeds!
  He shall love me without guile,
And to *him* I will discover
  The swan's nest among the reeds.

'And the steed shall be red-roan,
And the lover shall be noble,
  With an eye that takes the breath;
  And the lute he plays upon,
Shall strike ladies into trouble,
  As his sword strikes men to death.

'And the steed it shall be shod
All in silver, housed in azure,
  And the mane shall swim the wind;
  And the hoofs along the sod
Shall flash onward and keep measure,
  Till the shepherds look behind.

VII

'But my lover will not prize
All the glory that he rides in,
   When he gazes in my face.
   He will say, "O Love, thine eyes
Build the shrine my soul abides in,
   And I kneel here for thy grace."

VIII

'Then, aye, then – he shall kneel low,
With the red-roan steed anear him,
   Which shall seem to understand –
   Till I answer, "Rise and go!
For the world must love and fear him
   Whom I gift with heart and hand."

IX

'Then he will arise so pale,
I shall feel my own lips tremble
  With a *yes* I must not say,
    Nathless maiden-brave, "Farewell,"
I will utter, and dissemble –
    "Light to-morrow with to-day."

X

'Then he'll ride among the hills
To the wide world past the river,
  There to put away all wrong,
    To make straight distorted wills,
And to empty the broad quiver
  Which the wicked bear along.

XI

'Three times shall a young foot-page
Swim the stream and climb the mountain
    And kneel down beside my feet –
    "Lo, my master sends this gage,
Lady, for thy pity's counting!
    What wilt thou exchange for it?"

XII

'And the first time, I will send
A white rosebud for a guerdon, –
    And the second time, a glove;
    But the third time – I may bend
From my pride, and answer – "Pardon,
    If he comes to take my love."

XIII

'Then the young foot-page will run –
Then my lover will ride faster,
  Till he kneeleth at my knee:
  "I am a duke's eldest son!
Thousand serfs do call me master, –
  But, O Love, I love but *thee*!"

XIV

'He will kiss me on the mouth
Then, and lead me as a lover
  Through the crowds that praise his deeds:
  And, when soul-tied by one troth,
Unto *him* I will discover
  That swan's nest among the reeds.'

XV

Little Ellie, with her smile
Not yet ended, rose up gaily,
   Tied the bonnet, donned the shoe,
   And went homeward, round a mile,
Just to see, as she did daily,
   What more eggs were with the two.

XVI

Pushing through the elm-tree copse,
Winding up the stream, light-hearted,
   Where the osier pathway leads –
   Past the boughs she stoops – and stops.
Lo, the wild swan had deserted,
   And a rat had gnawed the reeds.

Ellie went home sad and slow.
If she found the lover ever,
   With his red-roan steed of steeds,
   Sooth I know not! but I know
She could never show him – never,
   That swan's nest among the reeds!

TO FLUSH, MY DOG

I

Loving friend, the gift of one
Who her own true faith has run
   Through thy lower nature,
Be my benediction said
With my hand upon thy head,
   Gentle fellow creature!

II

Like a lady's ringlets brown,
Flow thy silken ears adown
   Either side demurely
Of thy silver-suited breast,
Shining out from all the rest
   Of thy body purely.

III

Darkly brown thy body is,
Till the sunshine striking this
    Alchemize its dullness,
When the sleek curls manifold
Flash all over into gold,
    With a burnished fullness.

IV

Underneath my stroking hand,
Startled eyes of hazel bland
    Kindling, growing larger,
Up thou leapest with a spring,
Full of prank and curveting,
    Leaping like a charger.

V

Leap! thy broad tail waves a light,
Leap! thy slender feet are bright,
   Canopied in fringes;
Leap – those tasselled ears of thine
Flicker strangely, fair and fine,
   Down their golden inches.

VI

Yet, my pretty, sportive friend,
Little is 't to such an end
   That I praise thy rareness!
Other dogs may be thy peers
Haply in these drooping ears,
   And this glossy fairness.

VII

But of *thee* it shall be said,
This dog watched beside a bed
   Day and night unweary, –
Watched within a curtained room,
Where no sunbeam brake the gloom
   Round the sick and dreary.

VIII

Roses, gathered for a vase,
In that chamber died apace,
   Beam and breeze resigning;
This dog only, waited on,
Knowing that when light is gone
   Love remains for shining.

IX

Other dogs in thymy dew
Tracked the hares and followed through
   Sunny moor or meadow;
This dog only, crept and crept
Next a languid cheek that slept,
   Sharing in the shadow.

X

Other dogs of loyal cheer
Bounded at the whistle clear,
   Up the woodside hieing;
This dog only, watched in reach
Of a faintly uttered speech,
   Or a louder sighing.

XI

And if one or two quick tears
Dropped upon his glossy ears,
   Or a sign came double, –
Up he sprang in eager haste,
Fawning, fondling, breathing fast,
   In a tender trouble.

XII

And this dog was satisfied
If a pale thin hand would glide
   Down his dewlaps sloping, –
Which he pushed his nose within,
After, – platforming his chin
   On the palm left open.

XIII

This dog, if a friendly voice
Call him now to blyther choice
  Than such chamber-keeping,
'Come out!' praying from the door, –
Presseth backward as before,
  Up against me leaping.

XIV

Therefore to this dog will I,
Tenderly not scornfully,
  Render praise and favour:
With my hand upon his head,
Is my benediction said
  Therefore, and for ever.

XV

And because he loves me so,
Better than his kind will do
   Often, man or woman,
Give I back more love again
Than dogs often take of men,
   Leaning from my Human.

XVI

Blessings on thee, dog of mine,
Pretty collars make thee fine,
   Sugared milk make fat thee!
Pleasures wag on in thy tail,
Hands of gentle motion fail
   Nevermore, to pat thee!

XVII

Downy pillow take thy head,
Silken coverlid bestead,
　　Sunshine help thy sleeping!
No fly's buzzing wake thee up,
No man break thy purple cup,
　　Set for drinking deep in.

XVIII

Whiskered cats arointed flee,
Sturdy stoppers keep from thee
　　Cologne distillations;
Nuts lie in thy path for stones,
And thy feast-day macaroons
　　Turn to daily rations!

33

XIX

Mock I thee, in wishing weal? –
Tears are in my eyes to feel
    Thou art made so straitly,
Blessing needs must straiten too, –
Little canst thou joy or do,
    Thou who lovest *greatly*.

XX

Yet be blessèd to the height
Of all good and all delight
    Pervious to thy nature;
Only *loved* beyond that line,
With a love that answers thine,
    Loving fellow creature!

CATARINA TO CAMOENS

Dying in his absence abroad, and referring to the poem in
which he recorded the sweetness of her eyes

I

On the door you will not enter,
    I have gazed too long – adieu!
Hope withdraws her peradventure –
    Death is near me, – and not *you*.
        Come, O lover,
        Close and cover
These poor eyes, you called, I ween,
'Sweetest eyes, were ever seen.'

II

When I heard you sing that burden
    In my vernal days and bowers,
Other praises disregarding,
    I but hearkened that of yours –
        Only saying
        In heart-playing,
'Blessed eyes mine eyes have been,
If the sweetest, HIS have seen!'

III

But all changes. At this vesper,
   Cold the sun shines down the door.
If you stood there, would you whisper
   'Love, I love you,' as before, –
      Death pervading
      Now, and shading
Eyes you sang of, that yestreen,
As the sweetest ever seen?

IV

Yes, I think, were you beside them,
   Near the bed I die upon, –
Though their beauty you denied them,
   As you stood there, looking down,
      You would truly
      Call them duly,
For the love's sake found therein, –
'Sweetest eyes, were ever seen.'

V

And if *you* looked down upon them,
   And if *they* looked up to *you*,
All the light which has foregone them
   Would be gathered back anew.
         They would truly
         Be as duly
Love-transformed to beauty's sheen, –
'Sweetest eyes, were ever seen.'

VI

But, ah me! you only see me,
   In your thoughts of loving man,
Smiling soft perhaps and dreamy
   Through the wavings of my fan, –
         And unweeting
         Go repeating,
In your reverie serene,
'Sweetest eyes, were ever seen.'

VII

While my spirit leans and reaches
　　From my body still and pale,
Fain to hear what tender speech is
　　In your love to help my bale –
　　　　O my poet,
　　　　Come and show it!
Come, of latest love, to glean
'Sweetest eyes, were ever seen.'

VIII

O my poet, O my prophet,
　　When you praised their sweetness so,
Did you think, in singing of it,
　　That it might be near to go?
　　　　Had you fancies
　　　　From their glances,
That the grave would quickly screen
'Sweetest eyes, were ever seen'?

No reply! the fountain's warble
  In the court-yard sounds alone.
As the water to the marble
  So my heart falls with a moan
    From love-sighing
    To this dying.
Death forerunneth Love to win
'Sweetest eyes, were ever seen.'

X

Will you come! When I'm departed
  Where all sweetnesses are hid;
Where thy voice, my tender-hearted,
  Will not lift up either lid.
    Cry, O lover,
    Love is over!
Cry beneath the cypress green –
'Sweetest eyes, were ever seen.'

XI

When the angelus is ringing,
  Near the convent will you walk,
And recall the choral singing
  Which brought angels down our talk?
      Spirit-shriven
      I viewed Heaven,
Till you smiled – 'Is earth unclean,
Sweetest eyes, were ever seen?'

XII

When beneath the palace-lattice,
  You ride slow as you have done,
And you see a face there – that is
  Not the old familiar one, –
      Will you oftly
      Murmur softly,
'Here, ye watched me morn and e'en,
Sweetest eyes, were ever seen'?

XIII

When the palace-ladies, sitting
   Round your gittern, shall have said,
'Poet, sing those verses written
   For the lady who is dead,'
      Will you tremble,
      Yet dissemble, –
Or sing hoarse, with tears between,
'Sweetest eyes, were ever seen'?

XIV

'Sweetest eyes!' how sweet in flowings
   The repeated cadence is!
Though you sang a hundred poems,
   Still the best one would be this.
      I can hear it
      'Twixt my spirit
And the earth-noise intervene –
'Sweetest eyes, were ever seen!'

XV

But the priest waits for the praying,
    And the choir are on their knees,
And the soul must pass away in
    Strains more solemn high than these.
       Miserere
       For the weary!
Oh, no longer for Catrine,
'Sweetest eyes, were ever seen!'

XVI

Keep my ribbon, take and keep it
    (I have loosed it from my hair),
Feeling, while you overweep it,
    Not alone in your despair,
       Since with saintly
       Watch unfaintly
Out of heaven shall o'er you lean
'Sweetest eyes, were ever seen.'

XVII

But – but *now* – yet unremovèd
    Up to Heaven, they glisten fast.
You may cast away, Belovèd,
    In your future all my past.
        Such old phrases
        May be praises
For some fairer bosom-queen –
'Sweetest eyes, were ever seen!'

XVIII

Eyes of mine, what are ye doing?
    Faithless, faithless, – praised amiss
If a tear be of your showing,
    Dropt for any hope of HIS!
        Death has boldness
        Besides coldness,
If unworthy tears demean
'Sweetest eyes, were ever seen.'

XIX

I will look out to his future;
   I will bless it till it shine.
Should he ever be a suitor
   Unto sweeter eyes than mine,
      Sunshine gild them,
      Angels shield them,
Whatsoever eyes terrene
Be the sweetest HIS have seen!

A WOMAN'S SHORTCOMINGS

I

She has laughed as softly as if she sighed,
  She has counted six, and over,
Of a purse well filled, and a heart well tried –
  Oh, each a worthy lover!
They 'give her time'; for her soul must slip
  Where the world has set the grooving.
She will lie to none with her fair red lip –
  But love seeks truer loving.

II

She trembles her fan in a sweetness dumb,
  As her thoughts were beyond recalling,
With a glance for *one*, and a glance for *some*,
  From her eyelids rising and falling;
Speaks common words with a blushful air,
  Hears bold words, unreproving;
But her silence says – what she never will swear –
  And love seeks better loving.

III

Go, lady, lean to the night-guitar,
   And drop a smile to the bringer,
Then smile as sweetly, when he is far,
   At the voice of an indoor singer.
Bask tenderly beneath tender eyes;
   Glance lightly, on their removing;
And join new vows to old perjuries –
   But dare not call it loving.

IV

Unless you can think, when the song is done,
   No other is soft in the rhythm;
Unless you can feel, when left by One,
   That all men else go with him;
Unless you can know, when upraised by his breath,
   That your beauty itself wants proving;
Unless you can swear, 'For life, for death!' –
   Oh, fear to call it loving!

V

Unless you can muse in a crowd all day
   On the absent face that fixed you;
Unless you can love, as the angels may,
   With the breadth of heaven betwixt you;
Unless you can dream that his faith is fast,
   Through behoving and unbehoving;
Unless you can *die* when the dream is past –
   Oh, never call it loving!

A MAN'S REQUIREMENTS

I

Love me, sweet, with all thou art,
    Feeling, thinking, seeing, –
Love me in the lightest part,
    Love me in full being.

II

Love me with thine open youth
    In its frank surrender;
With the vowing of thy mouth,
    With its silence tender.

III

Love me with thine azure eyes,
    Made for earnest granting!
Taking colour from the skies,
    Can Heaven's truth be wanting?

IV

Love me with their lids, that fall
  Snow-like at first meeting;
Love me with thine heart, that all
  The neighbours then see beating.

V

Love me with thine hand stretched out
  Freely – open-minded;
Love me with thy loitering foot, –
  Hearing one behind it.

VI

Love me with thy voice, that turns
  Sudden faint above me;
Love me with thy blush that burns
  When I murmur, *Love me!*

VII

Love me with thy thinking soul –
  Break it to love-sighing;
Love me with thy thoughts that roll
  On through living – dying.

VIII

Love me in thy gorgeous airs,
  When the world has crowned thee!
Love me, kneeling at thy prayers, ·
  With the angels round thee.

IX

Love me pure, as musers do,
  Up the woodlands shady;
Love me gaily, fast, and true,
  As a winsome lady.

X

Through all hopes that keep us brave,
    Further off or nigher,
Love me for the house and grave, –
    And for something higher.

XI

Thus, if thou wilt prove me, dear,
    Woman's love no fable,
I will love *thee* – half-a-year –
    As a man is able.

A DENIAL

I

We have met late – it is too late to meet,
  O friend, not more than friend!
Death's forecome shroud is tangled round my feet,
And if I step or stir, I touch the end.
  In this last jeopardy
Can I approach thee, I, who cannot move?
How shall I answer thy request for love?
  Look in my face and see.

II

I love thee not, I dare not love thee! go
  In silence; drop my hand.
If thou seek roses, seek them where they blow
In garden-alleys, not in desert-sand.
  Can life and death agree,
That thou shouldst stoop thy song to my complaint?
I cannot love thee. If the word is faint,
  Look in my face and see.

I might have loved thee in some former days.
    Oh, then, my spirits had leapt
As now they sink, at hearing thy love-praise.
Before these faded cheeks were over-wept,
    Had this been asked of me,
To love thee with my whole strong heart and head, –
I should have said still . . . yes, but *smiled* and said,
    'Look in my face and see!'

But now . . . God sees me, God, who took my heart
    And drowned it in life's surge.
In all your wide warm earth I have no part –
A light song overcomes me like a dirge.
    Could Love's great harmony
The saints keep step to when their bonds are loose,
Not weigh me down? am *I* a wife to choose?
    Look in my face and see.

V

While I behold, as plain as one who dreams,
    Some woman of full worth,
Whose voice, as cadenced as a silver stream's,
Shall prove the fountain-soul which sends it forth;
    One younger, more thought-free
And fair and gay, than I, thou must forget,
With brighter eyes than these . . . which are not wet . . .
    Look in my face and see!

VI

So farewell thou, whom I have known too late
    To let thee come so near.
Be counted happy while men call thee great,
And one belovèd woman feels thee dear! –
    Not I! – that cannot be.
I am lost, I am changed, – I must go farther, where
The change shall take me worse, and no one dare
    Look in my face to see.

Meantime I bless thee. By these thoughts of mine
   I bless thee from all such!
I bless thy lamp to oil, thy cup to wine,
Thy hearth to joy, thy hand to an equal touch
   Of loyal troth. For me,
I love thee not, I love thee not! – away!
Here's no more courage in my soul to say
   'Look in my face and see.'

From SONNETS FROM THE PORTUGUESE

I

I thought once how Theocritus had sung
Of the sweet years, the dear and wished-for years,
Who each one in a gracious hand appears
To bear a gift for mortals, old or young:
And, as I mused it in his antique tongue,
I saw, in gradual vision through my tears,
The sweet, sad years, the melancholy years,
Those of my own life, who by turns had flung
A shadow across me. Straightway I was 'ware,
So weeping, how a mystic Shape did move
Behind me, and drew me backward by the hair,
And a voice said in mastery while I strove, . . .
'Guess now who holds thee?' – 'Death,' I said. But,
   there,
The silver answer rang, . . . 'Not Death, but Love.'

Unlike are we, unlike, O princely Heart!
Unlike our uses and our destinies.
Our ministering two angels look surprise
On one another, as they strike athwart
Their wings in passing. Thou, bethink thee, art
A guest for queens to social pageantries,
With gages from a hundred brighter eyes
Than tears even can make mine, to ply thy part
Of chief musician. What hast *thou* to do
With looking from the lattice-lights at me,
A poor, tired, wandering singer, . . . singing through
The dark, and leaning up a cypress tree?
The chrism is on thine head, – on mine, the dew, –
And Death must dig the level where these agree.

IV

Thou hast thy calling to some palace-floor,
Most gracious singer of high poems! where
The dancers will break footing, from the care
Of watching up thy pregnant lips for more.
And dost thou lift this house's latch too poor
For hand of thine? and canst thou think and bear
To let thy music drop here unaware
In folds of golden fullness at my door?
Look up and see the casement broken in,
The bats and owlets builders in the roof!
My cricket chirps against thy mandolin.
Hush, call no echo up in further proof
Of desolation! there's a voice within
That weeps . . . as thou must sing . . . alone, aloof.

VI

Go from me. Yet I feel that I shall stand
Henceforward in thy shadow. Nevermore
Alone upon the threshold of my door
Of individual life, I shall command
The uses of my soul, nor lift my hand
Serenely in the sunshine as before,
Without the sense of that which I forbore, . . .
Thy touch upon the palm. The widest land
Doom takes to part us, leaves thy heart in mine
With pulses that beat double. What I do
And what I dream include thee, as the wine
Must taste of its own grapes. And when I sue
God for myself, He hears that name of thine,
And sees within my eyes the tears of two.

What can I give thee back, O liberal
And princely giver, who hast brought the gold
And purple of thine heart, unstained, untold,
And laid them on the outside of the wall
For such as I to take or leave withal,
In unexpected largesse? am I cold,
Ungrateful, that for these most manifold
High gifts, I render nothing back at all?
Not so; not cold, – but very poor instead.
Ask God who knows. For frequent tears have run
The colours from my life, and left so dead
And pale a stuff, it were not fitly done
To give the same as pillow to thy head.
Go farther! let it serve to trample on.

Can it be right to give what I can give?
To let thee sit beneath the fall of tears
As salt as mine, and hear the sighing years
Re-sighing on my lips renunciative
Through those infrequent smiles which fail to live
For all thy adjurations? O my fears,
That this can scarce be right! We are not peers,
So to be lovers; and I own, and grieve,
That givers of such gifts as mine are, must
Be counted with the ungenerous. Out, alas!
I will not soil thy purple with my dust,
Nor breathe my poison on thy Venice-glass,
Nor give thee any love . . . which were unjust.
Beloved, I only love thee! let it pass.

If thou must love me, let it be for nought
Except for love's sake only. Do not say
'I love her for her smile . . . her look . . . her way
Of speaking gently, . . . for a trick of thought
That falls in well with mine, and certes brought
A sense of pleasant ease on such a day' –
For these things in themselves, Belovèd, may
Be changed, or change for thee, – and love, so
    wrought,
May be unwrought so. Neither love me for
Thine own dear pity's wiping my cheeks dry, –
A creature might forget to weep, who bore
Thy comfort long, and lose thy love thereby!
But love me for love's sake, that evermore
Thou mayst love on, through love's eternity.

I never gave a lock of hair away
To a man, dearest, except this to thee,
Which now upon my fingers thoughtfully
I ring out to the full brown length and say
'Take it.' My day of youth went yesterday;
My hair no longer bounds to my foot's glee,
Nor plant I it from rose or myrtle-tree,
As girls do, any more. It only may
Now shade on two pale cheeks, the mark of tears,
Taught drooping from the head that hangs aside
Through sorrow's trick. I thought the funeral-shears
Would take this first, but Love is justified, –
Take it, thou, . . . finding pure, from all those years,
The kiss my mother left here when she died.

When our two souls stand up erect and strong,
Face to face, silent, drawing nigh and nigher,
Until the lengthening wings break into fire
At either curvèd point, – what bitter wrong
Can the earth do to us, that we should not long
Be here contented? Think. In mounting higher,
The angels would press on us, and aspire
To drop some golden orb of perfect song
Into our deep, dear silence. Let us stay
Rather on earth, Belovèd, – where the unfit
Contrarious moods of men recoil away
And isolate pure spirits, and permit
A place to stand and love in for a day,
With darkness and the death-hour rounding it.

Is it indeed so? If I lay here dead,
Wouldst thou miss any life in losing mine?
And would the sun for thee more coldly shine,
Because of grave-damps falling round my head?
I marvelled, my Belovèd, when I read
Thy thought so in the letter. I am thine –
But . . . *so* much to thee? Can I pour thy wine
While my hands tremble? Then my soul, instead
Of dreams of death, resumes life's lower range.
Then, love me, Love! look on me . . . breathe on
   me!
As brighter ladies do not count it strange,
For love, to give up acres and degree,
I yield the grave for thy sake, and exchange
My near sweet view of Heaven, for earth with thee!

My letters! all dead paper . . . mute and white!
And yet they seem alive and quivering
Against my tremulous hands which loose the string
And let them drop down on my knee to-night.
This said, . . . he wished to have me in his sight
Once, as a friend: this fixed a day in spring
To come and touch my hand . . . a simple thing,
Yet I wept for it! – this, . . . the paper's light . . .
Said, *Dear, I love thee*; and I sank and quailed
As if God's future thundered on my past.
This said, *I am thine* – and so its ink has paled
With lying at my heart that beat too fast.
And this . . . O Love, thy words have ill availed,
If, what this said, I dared repeat at last!

Thou comest! all is said without a word.
I sit beneath thy looks, as children do
In the noon-sun, with souls that tremble through
Their happy eyelids from an unaverred
Yet prodigal inward joy. Behold, I erred
In that last doubt! and yet I cannot rue
The sin most, but the occasion . . . that we two
Should for a moment stand unministered
By a mutual presence. Ah, keep near and close,
Thou dovelike help! and, when my fears would rise,
With thy broad heart serenely interpose.
Brood down with thy divine sufficiencies
These thoughts which tremble when bereft of those,
Like callow birds left desert to the skies.

The first time that the sun rose on thine oath
To love me, I looked forward to the moon
To slacken all those bonds which seemed too soon
And quickly tied to make a lasting troth.
Quick-loving hearts, I thought, may quickly loathe;
And, looking on myself, I seemed not one
For such man's love! – more like an out of tune
Worn viol, a good singer would be wroth
To spoil his song with, and which, snatched in haste,
Is laid down at the first ill-sounding note.
I did not wrong myself so, but I placed
A wrong on *thee*. For perfect strains may float
'Neath master-hands, from instruments defaced, –
And great souls, at one stroke, may do and dote.

XXXV

If I leave all for thee, wilt thou exchange
And be all to me? Shall I never miss
Home-talk and blessing and the common kiss
That comes to each in turn, nor count it strange,
When I look up, to drop on a new range
Of walls and floors . . . another home than this?
Nay, wilt thou fill that place by me which is
Filled by dead eyes too tender to know change?
That's hardest. If to conquer love, has tried,
To conquer grief, tries more . . . as all things prove;
For grief indeed is love and grief beside.
Alas, I have grieved so I am hard to love.
Yet love me – wilt thou? Open thine heart wide,
And fold within, the wet wings of thy dove.

Because thou hast the power and own'st the grace
To look through and behind this mask of me
(Against which years have beat thus blanchingly
With their rains) and behold my soul's true face,
The dim and weary witness of life's race! –
Because thou hast the faith and love to see,
Through that same soul's distracting lethargy,
The patient angel waiting for a place
In the new heavens! because nor sin nor woe,
Nor God's infliction, nor death's neighbourhood,
Nor all which others viewing, turn to go, . . .
Nor all which makes me tired of all, self-viewed, . . .
Nothing repels thee, . . . dearest, teach me so
To pour out gratitude, as thou dost, good.

XLIII

How do I love thee? Let me count the ways.
I love thee to the depth and breadth and height
My soul can reach, when feeling out of sight.
For the ends of Being and ideal Grace.
I love thee to the level of every day's
Most quiet need, by sun and candlelight.
I love thee freely, as men strive for Right;
I love thee purely, as they turn from Praise.
I love thee with the passion put to use
In my old griefs, and with my childhood's faith.
I love thee with a love I seemed to lose
With my lost saints, – I love thee with the breath,
Smiles, tears, of all my life! – and, if God choose,
I shall but love thee better after death.

Belovèd, thou hast brought me many flowers
Plucked in the garden, all the summer through
And winter, and it seemed as if they grew
In this close room, nor missed the sun and showers.
So, in the like name of that love of ours,
Take back these thoughts which here unfolded too,
And which on warm and cold days I withdrew
From my heart's ground. Indeed, those beds and bowers
Be overgrown with bitter weeds and rue,
And wait thy weeding; yet here's eglantine,
Here's ivy! – take them, as I used to do
Thy flowers, and keep them where they shall not pine.
Instruct thine eyes to keep their colours true,
And tell thy soul, their roots are left in mine.

THE SOUL'S EXPRESSION

With stammering lips and insufficient sound
I strive and struggle to deliver right
That music of my nature, day and night
With dream and thought and feeling interwound,
And inly answering all the senses round
With octaves of a mystic depth and height
Which step out grandly to the infinite
From the dark edges of the sensual ground!
This song of soul I struggle to outbear
Through portals of the sense, sublime and whole,
And utter all myself into the air.
But if I did it, – as the thunder-roll
Breaks its own cloud, my flesh would perish there,
Before that dread apocalypse of soul.

AN APPREHENSION

If all the gentlest-hearted friends I know
Concentred in one heart their gentleness,
That still grew gentler, till its pulse was less
For life than pity, – I should yet be slow
To bring my own heart nakedly below
The palm of such a friend, that he should press
Motive, condition, means, appliances,
My false ideal joy and fickle woe,
Out full to light and knowledge; I should fear
Some plait between the brows – some rougher chime
In the free voice . . . O angels, let your flood
Of bitter scorn dash on me! do ye hear
What *I* say, who bear calmly all the time
This everlasting face to face with GOD?

GRIEF

I tell you, hopeless grief is passionless;
That only men incredulous of despair,
Half-taught in anguish, through the midnight air
Beat upward to God's throne in loud access
Of shrieking and reproach. Full desertness
In souls, as countries, lieth silent-bare
Under the blanching, vertical eye-glare
Of the absolute Heavens. Deep-hearted man, express
Grief for thy Dead in silence like to death: –
Most like a monumental statue set
In everlasting watch and moveless woe,
Till itself crumble to the dust beneath.
Touch it: the marble eyelids are not wet;
If it could weep, it could arise and go.

From AURORA LEIGH
First book

Of writing many books there is no end;
And I who have written much in prose and verse
For others' uses, will write now for mine, –
Will write my story for my better self,
As when you paint your portrait for a friend,
Who keeps it in a drawer and looks at it
Long after he has ceased to love you, just
To hold together what he was and is.
I, writing thus, am still what men call young;
I have not so far left the coasts of life
To travel inward, that I cannot hear
That murmur of the outer Infinite
Which unweaned babies smile at in their sleep
When wondered at for smiling; not so far,
But still I catch my mother at her post
Beside the nursery door, with finger up,
"Hush, hush – here's too much noise!" while her sweet
    eyes
Leap forward, taking part against her word
In the child's riot. Still I sit and feel
My father's slow hand, when she had left us both,
Stroke out my childish curls across his knee,

And hear Assunta's daily jest (she knew
He liked it better than a better jest)
Inquire how many golden scudi went
To make such ringlets. O my father's hand,
Stroke heavily, heavily the poor hair down,
Draw, press the child's head closer to thy knee!
I'm still too young, too young, to sit alone.

I write. My mother was a Florentine,
Whose rare blue eyes were shut from seeing me
When scarcely I was four years old, my life
A poor spark snatched up from a failing lamp
Which went out therefore. She was weak and frail;
She could not bear the joy of giving life,
The mother's rapture slew her. If her kiss
Had left a longer weight upon my lips
It might have steadied the uneasy breath,
And reconciled and fraternised my soul
With the new order. As it was, indeed,
I felt a mother-want about the world,
And still went seeking, like a bleating lamb
Left out at night in shutting up the fold, –

As restless as a nest-deserted bird
Grown chill through something being away, though
    what
It knows not. I, Aurora Leigh, was born
To make my father sadder, and myself
Not overjoyous, truly. Women know
The way to rear up children (to be just),
They know a simple, merry, tender knack
Of tying sashes, fitting baby-shoes,
And stringing pretty words that make no sense,
And kissing full sense into empty words,
Which things are corals to cut life upon,
Although such trifles: children learn by such,
Love's holy earnest in a pretty play
And get not over-early solemnised,
But seeing, as in a rose-bush, Love's Divine
Which burns and hurts not, – not a single bloom, –
Become aware and unafraid of Love.
Such good do mothers. Fathers love as well
 – Mine did, I know, – but still with heavier brains,
And wills more consciously responsible,
And not as wisely, since less foolishly;
So mothers have God's license to be missed.

My father was an austere Englishman,
Who, after a dry lifetime spent at home
In college-learning, law, and parish talk,
Was flooded with a passion unaware,
His whole provisioned and complacent past
Drowned out from him that moment. As he stood
In Florence, where he had come to spend a month
And note the secret of Da Vinci's drains,
He musing somewhat absently perhaps
Some English question . . . whether men should pay
The unpopular but necessary tax
With left or right hand – in the alien sun
In that great square of the Santissima
There drifted past him (scarcely marked enough
To move his comfortable island scorn)
A train of priestly banners, cross and psalm,
The white-veiled rose-crowned maidens holding up
Tall tapers, weighty for such wrists, aslant
To the blue luminous tremor of the air,
And letting drop the white wax as they went
To eat the bishop's wafer at the church;
From which long trail of chanting priests and girls,
A face flashed like a cymbal on his face
And shook with silent clangour brain and heart,

Transfiguring him to music. Thus, even thus,
He too received his sacramental gift
With eucharistic meanings; for he loved.

And thus beloved, she died. I've heard it said
That but to see him in the first surprise
Of widower and father, nursing me,
Unmothered little child of four years old,
His large man's hands afraid to touch my curls,
As if the gold would tarnish, – his grave lips
Contriving such a miserable smile
As if he knew needs must, or I should die,
And yet 'twas hard, – would almost make the stones
Cry out for pity. There's a verse he set
In Santa Croce to her memory, –
'Weep for an infant too young to weep much
When death removed this mother' – stops the mirth
To-day on women's faces when they walk
With rosy children hanging on their gowns,
Under the cloister to escape the sun
That scorches in the piazza. After which
He left our Florence and made haste to hide
Himself, his prattling child, and silent grief,
Among the mountains above Pelago;
Because unmothered babes, he thought, had need

Of mother nature more than others use,
And Pan's white goats, with udders warm and full
Of mystic contemplations, come to feed
Poor milkless lips of orphans like his own –
Such scholar-scraps he talked, I've heard from friends,
For even prosaic men who wear grief long
Will get to wear it as a hat aside
With a flower stuck in't. Father, then, and child,
We lived among the mountains many years,
God's silence on the outside of the house,
And we who did not speak too loud within,
And old Assunta to make up the fire,
Crossing herself whene'er a sudden flame
Which lightened from the firewood, made alive
That picture of my mother on the wall.

The painter drew it after she was dead,
And when the face was finished, throat and hands,
Her cameriera carried him, in hate
Of the English-fashioned shroud, the last brocade
She dressed in at the Pitti; 'he should paint
No sadder thing than that,' she swore, 'to wrong
Her poor signora.' Therefore very strange
The effect was. I, a little child, would crouch
For hours upon the floor with knees drawn up,

And gaze across them, half in terror, half
In adoration, at the picture there, –
That swan-like supernatural white life
Just sailing upward from the red stiff silk
Which seemed to have no part in it nor power
To keep it from quite breaking out of bounds.
For hours I sat and stared. Assunta's awe
And my poor father's melancholy eyes
Still pointed that way. That way went my thoughts
When wandering beyond sight. And as I grew
In years, I mixed, confused, unconsciously,
Whatever I last read or heard or dreamed,
Abhorrent, admirable, beautiful,
Pathetical, or ghastly, or grotesque,
With still that face . . . which did not therefore change,
But kept the mystic level of all forms,
Hates, fears, and admirations, was by turns
Ghost, fiend, and angel, fairy, witch, and sprite,
A dauntless Muse who eyes a dreadful Fate,
A loving Psyche who loses sight of Love,
A still Medusa with mild milky brows
All curdled and all clothed upon with snakes
Whose slime falls fast as sweat will; or anon
Our Lady of the Passion, stabbed with swords
Where the Babe sucked; or Lamia in her first

Moonlighted pallor, ere she shrunk and blinked
And shuddering wriggled down to the unclean;
Or my own mother, leaving her last smile
In her last kiss upon the baby-mouth
My father pushed down on the bed for that, –
Or my dead mother, without smile or kiss,
Buried at Florence. All which images,
Concentred on the picture, glassed themselves
Before my meditative childhood, as
The incoherencies of change and death
Are represented fully, mixed and merged,
In the smooth fair mystery of perpetual Life.

And while I stared away my childish wits
Upon my mother's picture (ah, poor child!),
My father, who through love had suddenly
Thrown off the old conventions, broken loose
From chin-bands of the soul, like Lazarus,
Yet had no time to learn to talk and walk
Or grow anew familiar with the sun, –
Who had reached to freedom, not to action, lived,
But lived as one entranced, with thoughts, not aims, –
Whom love had unmade from a common man
But not completed to an uncommon man, –
My father taught me what he had learnt the best

Before he died and left me, – grief and love.
And, seeing we had books among the hills,
Strong words of counselling souls confederate
With vocal pines and waters, – out of books
He taught me all the ignorance of men,
And how God laughs in heaven when any man
Says 'Here I'm learned; this, I understand;
In that, I am never caught at fault or doubt.'
He sent the schools to school, demonstrating
A fool will pass for such through one mistake,
While a philosopher will pass for such,
Through said mistakes being ventured in the gross
And heaped up to a system.
                                      I am like,
They tell me, my dear father. Broader brows
Howbeit, upon a slenderer undergrowth
Of delicate features, – paler, near as grave;
But then my mother's smile breaks up the whole,
And makes it better sometimes than itself.

So, nine full years, our days were hid with God
Among his mountains: I was just thirteen,
Still growing like the plants from unseen roots
In tongue-tied Springs, – and suddenly awoke
To full life and life's needs and agonies

With an intense, strong, struggling heart beside
A stone-dead father. Life, struck sharp on death,
Makes awful lightning. His last word was 'Love – '
'Love, my child, love, love!' – (then he had done with
   grief)
'Love, my child.' Ere I answered he was gone,
And none was left to love in all the world.
. . .

I think I see my father's sister stand
Upon the hall-step of her country-house
To give me welcome. She stood straight and calm,
Her somewhat narrow forehead braided tight
As if for taming accidental thoughts
From possible pulses; brown hair pricked with gray
By frigid use of life (she was not old,
Although my father's elder by a year),
A nose drawn sharply, yet in delicate lines;
A close mild mouth, a little soured about
The ends, through speaking unrequited loves
Or peradventure niggardly half-truths;
Eyes of no colour, – once they might have smiled,
But never, never have forgot themselves
In smiling; cheeks, in which was yet a rose
Of perished summers, like a rose in a book,

Kept more for ruth than pleasure, – if past bloom,
Past fading also.
                                    She had lived, we'll say,
A harmless life, she called a virtuous life,
A quiet life, which was not life at all
(But that, she had not lived enough to know),
Between the vicar and the county squires,
The lord-lieutenant looking down sometimes
From the empyrean to assure their souls
Against chance vulgarisms, and, in the abyss,
The apothecary, looked on once a year
To prove their soundness of humility.
The poor-club exercised her Christian gifts
Of knitting stockings, stitching petticoats,
Because we are of one flesh, after all,
And need one flannel (with a proper sense
Of difference in the quality) – and still
The book-club, guarded from your modern trick
Of shaking dangerous questions from the crease,
Preserved her intellectual. She had lived
A sort of cage-bird life, born in a cage,
Accounting that to leap from perch to perch
Was act and joy enough for any bird.
Dear heaven, how silly are the things that live
In thickets, and eat berries!

I, alas,
A wild bird scarcely fledged, was brought to her cage,
And she was there to meet me. Very kind.
Bring the clean water, give out the fresh seed.

She stood upon the steps to welcome me,
Calm, in black garb. I clung about her neck, –
Young babes, who catch at every shred of wool
To draw the new light closer, catch and cling
Less blindly. In my ears my father's word
Hummed ignorantly, as the sea in shells,
'Love, love, my child.' She, black there with my grief,
Might feel my love – she was his sister once –
I clung to her. A moment she seemed moved,
Kissed me with cold lips, suffered me to cling,
And drew me feebly through the hall into
The room she sat in.
                    There, with some strange spasm
Of pain and passion, she wrung loose my hands
Imperiously, and held me at arm's length,
And with two grey-steel naked-bladed eyes
Searched through my face, – aye, stabbed it through
    and through,
Through brows and cheeks and chin, as if to find
A wicked murderer in my innocent face,

If not here, there perhaps. Then, drawing breath,
She struggled for her ordinary calm –
And missed it rather, – told me not to shrink,
As if she had told me not to lie or swear, –
'She loved my father and would love me too
As long as I deserved it.' Very kind.

I understood her meaning afterward;
She thought to find my mother in my face,
And questioned it for that. For she, my aunt,
Had loved my father truly, as she could,
And hated, with the gall of gentle souls,
My Tuscan mother who had fooled away
A wise man from wise courses, a good man
From obvious duties, and, depriving her,
His sister, of the household precedence,
Had wronged his tenants, robbed his native land,
And made him mad, alike by life and death,
In love and sorrow. She had pored for years
What sort of woman could be suitable
To her sort of hate, to entertain it with,
And so, her very curiosity
Became hate too, and all the idealism
She ever used in life was used for hate,
Till hate, so nourished, did exceed at last

The love from which it grew, in strength and heat,
And wrinkled her smooth conscience with a sense
Of disputable virtue (say not, sin)
When Christian doctrine was enforced at church.

And thus my father's sister was to me
My mother's hater. From that day she did
Her duty to me (I appreciate it
In her own word as spoken to herself),
Her duty, in large measure, well pressed out
But measured always. She was generous, bland,
More courteous than was tender, gave me still
The first place, – as if fearful that God's saints
Would look down suddenly and say 'Herein
You missed a point, I think, through lack of love.'
Alas, a mother never is afraid
Of speaking angerly to any child,
Since love, she knows, is justified of love.
And I, I was a good child on the whole,
A meek and manageable child. Why not?
I did not live, to have the faults of life:
There seemed more true life in my father's grave
Than in all England. Since *that* threw me off
Who fain would cleave (his latest will, they say,
Consigned me to his land), I only thought

Of lying quiet there where I was thrown
Like sea-weed on the rocks, and suffering her
To prick me to a pattern with her pin,
Fibre from fibre, delicate leaf from leaf,
And dry out from my drowned anatomy
The last sea-salt left in me.

. . .

                           At first
I felt no life which was not patience, – did
The thing she bade me, without heed to a thing
Beyond it, sat in just the chair she placed,
With back against the window, to exclude
The sight of the great lime-tree on the lawn,
Which seemed to have come on purpose from the
    woods
To bring the house a message, – ay, and walked
Demurely in her carpeted low rooms,
As if I should not, hearkening my own steps,
Misdoubt I was alive. I read her books,
Was civil to her cousin, Romney Leigh,
Gave ear to her vicar, tea to her visitors,
And heard them whisper, when I changed a cup
(I blushed for joy at that), – 'The Italian child,
For all her blue eyes and her quiet ways,

Thrives ill in England: she is paler yet
Than when we came the last time; she will die.'

'Will die.' My cousin, Romney Leigh, blushed too,
With sudden anger, and approaching me
Said low between his teeth, 'You're wicked now?
You wish to die and leave the world a-dusk
For others, with your naughty light blown out?'
I looked into his face defyingly;
He might have known that, being what I was,
'Twas natural to like to get away
As far as dead folk can: and then indeed
Some people make no trouble when they die.
He turned and went abruptly, slammed the door,
And shut his dog out.

        Romney, Romney Leigh.
I have not named my cousin hitherto,
And yet I used him as a sort of friend;
My elder by few years, but cold and shy
And absent . . . tender, when he thought of it,
Which scarcely was imperative, grave betimes,
As well as early master of Leigh Hall,
Whereof the nightmare sat upon his youth,
Repressing all its seasonable delights,
And agonising with a ghastly sense

Of universal hideous want and wrong
To incriminate possession. When he came
From college to the country, very oft
He crossed the hill on visits to my aunt,
With gifts of blue grapes from the hothouses,
A book in one hand, – mere statistics (if
I chanced to lift the cover), count of all
The goats whose beards grow sprouting down toward
    hell
Against God's separative judgment-hour.
And she, she almost loved him, – even allowed
That sometimes he should seem to sigh my way;
It made him easier to be pitiful,
And sighing was his gift. So, undisturbed,
At whiles she let him shut my music up
And push my needles down, and lead me out
To see in that south angle of the house
The figs grow black as if by a Tuscan rock,
On some light pretext. She would turn her head
At other moments, go to fetch a thing,
And leave me breath enough to speak with him,
For his sake; it was simple.

                Sometimes too
He would have saved me utterly, it seemed,
He stood and looked so.

                Once, he stood so near,

He dropped a sudden hand upon my head
Bent down on woman's work, as soft as rain –
But then I rose and shook it off as fire,
The stranger's touch that took my father's place
Yet dared seem soft.

              I used him for a friend
Before I ever knew him for a friend.
'Twas better, 'twas worse also, afterward:
We came so close, we saw our differences
Too intimately. Always Romney Leigh
Was looking for the worms, I for the gods.
A godlike nature his; the gods look down,
Incurious of themselves; and certainly
'Tis well I should remember, how, those days,
I was a worm too, and he looked on me.

A little by his act perhaps, yet more
By something in me, surely not my will,
I did not die. But slowly, as one in swoon,
To whom life creeps back in the form of death,
With a sense of separation, a blind pain
Of blank obstruction, and a roar i' the ears
Of visionary chariots which retreat
As earth grows clearer . . . slowly, by degrees;
I woke, rose up . . . where was I? in the world;
For uses therefore I must count worth while.

LORD WALTER'S WIFE

I

'But why do you go,' said the lady, while both sate
  under the yew,
And her eyes were alive in their depth, as the kraken
  beneath the sea-blue.

II

'Because I fear you,' he answered; – 'because you are
  far too fair,
And able to strangle my soul in a mesh of your gold-
  coloured hair.'

III

'Oh, that,' she said, 'is no reason! Such knots are
  quickly undone,
And too much beauty, I reckon, is nothing but too
  much sun.'

IV

'Yet farewell so,' he answered; – 'the sunstroke's fatal
  at times.
I value your husband, Lord Walter, whose gallop rings
  still from the limes.'

V

'Oh, that,' she said, 'is no reason. You smell a rose
  through a fence:
If two should smell it, what matter? who grumbles, and
  where's the pretence?'

VI

'But I,' he replied, 'have promised another, when love
   was free,
To love her alone, alone, who alone and afar loves
   me.'

VII

'Why, that,' she said, 'is no reason. Love's always free,
   I am told.
Will you vow to be safe from the headache on
   Tuesday, and think it will hold?'

VIII

'But you,' he replied, 'have a daughter, a young little
    child, who was laid
In your lap to be pure; so I leave you: the angels
    would make me afraid.'

IX

'Oh, that,' she said, 'is no reason. The angels keep out
    of the way;
And Dora, the child, observes nothing, although you
    should please me and stay.'

X

At which he rose up in his anger, – 'Why, now, you
 no longer are fair!
Why, now, you no longer are fatal, but ugly and
 hateful, I swear.'

XI

At which she laughed out in her scorn. – 'These men!
 Oh, these men overnice,
Who are shocked if a colour not virtuous, is frankly
 put on by a vice.'

XII

Her eyes blazed upon him – 'And *you!* You bring us
    your vices so near
That we smell them! You think in our presence a
    thought 'twould defame us to hear!

XIII

'What reason had you, and what right, – I appeal to
    your soul from my life, –
To find me too fair as a woman? Why, sir, I am pure,
    and a wife.

XIV

'Is the day-star too fair up above you? It burns you
    not. Dare you imply
I brushed you more close than the star does, when
    Walter had set me as high?

XV

'If a man finds a woman too fair, he means simply
    adapted too much
To uses unlawful and fatal. The praise! – shall I thank
    you for such?

XVI

'Too fair? – not unless you misuse us! and surely if,
  once in a while,
You attain to it, straightway you call us no longer too
  fair, but too vile.

XVII

'A moment, – I pray your attention! – I have a poor
  word in my head
I must utter, though womanly custom would set it
  down better unsaid,

XVIII

'You grew, sir, pale to impertinence, once when I
  showed you a ring.
You kissed my fan when I dropped it. No matter! –
  I've broken the thing.

XIX

'You did me the honour, perhaps, to be moved at my
  side now and then
In the senses – a vice, I have heard, which is common
  to beasts and some men.

XX

'Love's a virtue for heroes! – as white as the snow on
  high hills,
And immortal as every great soul is that struggles,
  endures, and fulfils.

XXI

'I love my Walter profoundly, – you, Maude, though
  you faltered a week,
For the sake of . . . what was it? an eyebrow? or, less
  still, a mole on a cheek?

XXII

'And since, when all's said, you're too noble to stoop
    to the frivolous cant
About crimes irresistible, virtues that swindle, betray
    and supplant,

XXIII

'I determined to prove to yourself that, whate'er you
    might dream or avow
By illusion, you wanted precisely no more of me than
    you have now.

XXIV

'There! Look me full in the face! – in the face.
   Understand, if you can,
That the eyes of such women as I am, are clean as the
   palm of a man.

XXV

'Drop his hand, you insult him. Avoid us for fear we
   should cost you a scar –
You take us for harlots, I tell you, and not for the
   women we are.

XXVI

'You wronged me: but then I considered . . . there's
    Walter! And so at the end,
I vowed that he should not be mulcted, by me, in the
    hand of a friend.

XXVII

'Have I hurt you indeed? We are quits then. Nay,
    friend of my Walter, be mine!
Come Dora, my darling, my angel, and help me to ask
    him to dine.'

BIANCA AMONG THE NIGHTINGALES

I

The cypress stood up like a church
    That night we felt our love would hold,
And saintly moonlight seemed to search
    And wash the whole world clean as gold;
The olives crystallized the vales'
    Broad slopes until the hills grew strong:
The fireflies and the nightingales
    Throbbed each to either, flame and song.
The nightingales, the nightingales.

Upon the angle of its shade
    The cypress stood, self-balanced high;
Half up, half down, as double-made,
    Along the ground, against the sky.
And *we*, too! from such soul-height went
    Such leaps of blood, so blindly driven,
We scarce knew if our nature meant
    Most passionate earth or intense heaven.
The nightingales, the nightingales.

III

We paled with love, we shook with love,
    We kissed so close we could not vow;
Till Giulio whispered, 'Sweet above
    God's Ever guarantees this Now.'
And through his words the nightingales
    Drove straight and full their long clear call,
Like arrows through heroic mails,
    And love was awful in it all.
The nightingales, the nightingales.

IV

O cold white moonlight of the north,
    Refresh these pulses, quench this hell!
O coverture of death drawn forth
    Across this garden-chamber . . . well!
But what have nightingales to do
    In gloomy England, called the free.
(Yes, free to die in! . . .) when we two
    Are sundered, singing still to me?
And still they sing, the nightingales.

V

I think I hear him, how he cried
   'My own soul's life' between their notes.
Each man has but one soul supplied,
   And that's immortal. Though his throat's
On fire with passion now, to *her*
   He can't say what to me he said!
And yet he moves her, they aver.
   The nightingales sing through my head,
The nightingales, the nightingales.

He says to *her* what moves her most.
   He would not name his soul within
Her hearing, – rather pays her cost
   With praises to her lips and chin.
Man has but one soul, 'tis ordained,
   And each soul but one love, I add;
Yet souls are damned and love's profaned
   These nightingales will sing me mad!
The nightingales, the nightingales.

I marvel how the birds can sing.
   There's little difference, in their view,
Betwixt our Tuscan trees that spring
   As vital flames into the blue,
And dull round blots of foliage meant
   Like saturated sponges here
To suck the fogs up. As content
   Is *he* too in this land, 'tis clear.
And still they sing, the nightingales.

VIII

My native Florence! dear, forgone!
    I see across the Alpine ridge
How the last feast-day of Saint John
Shot rockets from Carraia bridge.
The luminous city, tall with fire,
    Trod deep down in that river of ours,
While many a boat with lamp and choir
    Skimmed birdlike over glittering towers.
I will not hear these nightingales.

I seem to float, *we* seem to float
   Down Arno's stream in festive guise;
A boat strikes flame into our boat,
   And up that lady seems to rise
As then she rose. The shock had flashed
   A vision on us! What a head,
What leaping eyeballs! – beauty dashed
   To splendour by a sudden dread.
And still they sing, the nightingales.

Too bold to sin, too weak to die;
    Such women are so. As for me,
I would we had drowned there, he and I,
    That moment, loving perfectly.
He had not caught her with her loosed
    Gold ringlets . . . rarer in the south . . .
Nor heard the 'Grazie tanto' bruised
    To sweetness by her English mouth.
And still they sing, the nightingales.

She had not reached him at my heart
    With her fine tongue, as snakes indeed
Kill flies; nor had I, for my part,
    Yearned after, in my desperate need,
And followed him as he did her
    To coasts left bitter by the tide,
Whose very nightingales, elsewhere
    Delighting, torture and deride!
For still they sing, the nightingales.

XII

A worthless woman! mere cold clay
 As all false things are! but so fair,
She takes the breath of men away
 Who gaze upon her unaware.
I would not play her larcenous tricks
 To have her looks! She lied and stole,
And spat into my love's pure pyx
 The rank saliva of her soul.
And still they sing, the nightingales.

I would not for her white and pink,
    Though such he likes – her grace of limb,
Though such he has praised – nor yet, I think,
    For life itself, though spent with him,
Commit such sacrilege, affront
    God's nature which is love, intrude
'Twixt two affianced souls, and hunt
    Like spiders, in the altar's wood.
I cannot bear these nightingales.

If she chose sin, some gentler guise
    She might have sinned in, so it seems:
She might have pricked out both my eyes,
    And I still seen him in my dreams!
 - Or drugged me in my soup or wine,
    Nor left me angry afterward:
To die here with his hand in mine
    His breath upon me, were not hard.
(Our Lady hush these nightingales!)

But set a springe for *him*, 'mio ben,'
   My only good, my first last love! –
Though Christ knows well what sin is, when
   He sees some things done they must move
Himself to wonder. Let her pass.
   I think of her by night and day.
Must *I* too join her . . . out, alas! . . .
   With Giulio, in each word I say?
And evermore the nightingales!

Giulio, my Giulio! – sing they so,
    And you be silent? Do I speak,
And you not hear? An arm you throw
    Round some one, and I feel so weak?
    – Oh, owl-like birds! They sing for spite,
    They sing for hate, they sing for doom!
They'll sing through death who sing through night,
    They'll sing and stun me in the tomb –
The nightingales, the nightingales!

AMY'S CRUELTY

I

Fair Amy of the terraced house,
  Assist me to discover
Why you who would not hurt a mouse
  Can torture so your lover.

II

You give your coffee to the cat,
  You stroke the dog for coming,
And all your face grows kinder at
  The little brown bee's humming.

III

But when *he* haunts your door . . . the town
  Marks coming and marks going . . .
You seem to have stitched your eyelids down
  To that long piece of sewing!

You never give a look, not you,
 Nor drop him a 'Good morning,'
To keep his long day warm and blue,
 So fretted by your scorning.

She shook her head – 'The mouse and bee
For crumb or flower will linger:
The dog is happy at my knee,
The cat purrs at my finger.

VI

'But *he* . . . to *him*, the least thing given
Means great things at a distance;
He wants my world, my sun, my heaven,
Soul, body, whole existence.

VII

'They say love gives as well as takes;
But I'm a simple maiden, –
My mother's first smile when she wakes
I still have smiled and prayed in.

VIII

'I only know my mother's love
Which gives all and asks nothing;
And this new loving sets the groove
Too much the way of loathing.

IX

'Unless he gives me all in change,
I forfeit all things by him:
The risk is terrible and strange –
I tremble, doubt, . . . deny him.

X

'He's sweetest friend, or hardest foe,
Best angel, or worst devil;
I either hate or . . . love him so,
I can't be merely civil!

XI

'You trust a woman who puts forth,
Her blossoms thick as summer's?
You think she dreams what love is worth,
Who casts it to new-comers?

XII

'Such love's a cowslip-ball to fling,
A moment's pretty pastime;
I give . . . all me, if anything,
The first time and the last time.

XIII

'Dear neighbour of the trellised house,
A man should murmur never,
Though treated worse than dog and mouse,
Till doted on for ever!'